LIFE
SCIENCE
STORIES

Adaptation and Survival

Louise and
Richard
Spilsbury

 **Gareth Stevens**
Publishing

Please visit our website, www.garethstevens.com. For a free color catalog of all our high-quality books, call toll free 1-800-542-2595 or fax 1-877-542-2596.

Library of Congress Cataloging-in-Publication Data

Spilsbury, Richard, 1963-
 Adaptation and survival / Richard Spilsbury.
    p. cm. — (Life science stories)
ISBN 978-1-4339-8700-7 (pbk.)
ISBN 978-1-4339-8701-4 (6-pack)
ISBN 978-1-4339-8699-4 (library binding)
1. Adaptation (Biology)—Anecdotes—Juvenile literature. 2. Animal defenses—Anecdotes–Juvenile literature. I. Title.
 QH546.S655 2013
 591.4—dc23

2012026472

Published in 2013 by
Gareth Stevens Publishing
111 East 14th Street, Suite 349
New York, NY 10003

© 2013 Gareth Stevens Publishing

Produced for Gareth Stevens by Calcium Creative Ltd
Designed by Paul Myerscough and Geoff Ward
Edited by Sarah Eason and Harriet McGregor

Picture credits: Cover: Shutterstock: Kjersti Joergense. Inside: Shutterstock: 312010 23, Johan Barnard 16, Sylvie Bouchard 20, Davidpstephens 6, Defpicture 14, Maria Dryfhout 24, FloridaStock 22, Joshua Haviv 7, Holbox 12, 13, Imageman 11, Jadimages 10, Javarman 29, Cathy Keifer 18, Peter Kirillov 21, Tamara Kulikova 15, Marcokenya 17, Rob McKay 11t, Pakul54 8, Przemyslaw 19, Becky Sheridan 28, Audrey Snider-Bell 25, Victor Soares 27, Brendan van Son 5, Jordan Tan 9, Tramper 4, Mogens Trolle 26, Visceralimage 11b.

Printed in the United States of America

CPSIA compliance information: Batch #CW 13GS: For further information contact Gareth Stevens, New York, New York at 1-800-542-2595.

Contents

Ways to Survive

Animals must change in order to stay alive in their **habitat**. This is called **adaptation**. The change could be to the animal's body or the way in which it behaves. Adaptations can help an animal to hunt, eat, move, find a **mate**, or protect itself. Different types of animals have adapted in different ways over thousands of years.

Meet the Mole

Moles have adaptations that help them to survive underground. They have sharp claws for digging tunnels in the soil. They also have a large nose to smell where earthworms are and sharp teeth to hold on to the worms when they catch them.

Can you see this mole's tiny eyes? Moles do not need to see well because they live in the dark.

This black male frigate bird has **inflated** its bright red throat pouch to get itself noticed!

THE FRIGATE BIRD

Frigate birds are adapted to life in the air. Their 6-foot (2 m) wingspan helps them swoop down to snatch fish from the ocean and fly off again. They are great flyers but cannot walk or swim well. They only land on cliffs to rest or find a mate. Male frigate birds have another amazing adaptation. They can blow up their red throat pouch like a balloon to attract a female!

Great White Killer

The great white shark is an awesome hunter and one of the most successful **predators** in the ocean. This enormous shark has many adaptations for hunting.

Fast and Furious

The great white shark has an amazing sense of smell. It can sense a single drop of blood in the water from 3 miles (5 km) away. Its torpedo-like body helps it to swim at speeds of up to 15 miles (24 km) per hour. Its powerful tail can push it upward so fast it can knock **prey** out of the water!

Great white sharks have 300 razor-sharp, jagged teeth to grab and tear prey. When teeth wear out, new ones grow in their place.

Survival Story

COLORED TO KILL

Great white sharks have a gray back and a white belly. This coloring is called countershading. It is a type of **camouflage**, an adaptation that helps the shark to sneak up on prey. The top half of the shark is dark. When prey look down from above, the shark blends in with the dark waters below. The bottom half is light. When prey look up from below, the shark blends in with the sunlit waters above it.

This shark's coloring means that by the time most animals realize the shark is near, it's too late!

Giraffe Meals

One of the giraffe's favorite foods are leaves from acacia trees. Acacia trees have hard, sharp thorns that stop most animals from eating them. So why can giraffes eat them?

Amazing Tongue

A giraffe's tongue is adapted to get around this thorny problem! It is 18 inches (46 cm) long and can reach around the acacia thorns to get to the leaves. The tongue grasps onto the leaves, then plucks them from the tree. The giraffe's mouth also makes lots of thick, sticky spit called saliva. This covers any thorns the giraffe might swallow to stop them from hurting the animal's insides.

Giraffes have purple and black tongues. Scientists think that this color protects their tongues from sunburn when reaching for leaves.

A giraffe's neck is around 6 feet (2 m) long. It has just seven bones in it—the same number found in the neck of a person. However, the giraffe's bones are much bigger—each is 10 inches (25 cm) long!

Survival Story

FOOD FIGHTS

There are lots of plant eaters in the grasslands where giraffes live. Giraffes have developed a long neck so they can eat leaves high in the trees, where most other plant eaters cannot reach. This adaptation means they do not have to **compete** with many other animals for food. Being tall also protects giraffes. From up high, they can see hungry lions up to 20 miles (32 km) away.

Owl Flight

The owl is an awesome nighttime hunter. It has adapted to fly almost silently through the air. Owls catch small animals on the ground. At night, these prey animals use sound to tell if a predator is near. Owls use the skill of silent flight to catch their prey.

Silent and Deadly

The owl is able to fly in silence because of the design of its feathers. Owls have large feathers with jagged edges that soften the sound of the flapping wing. The feathers are also coated in a velvety-smooth cover, which soaks up sound. This lets the owl silently swoop down on its prey.

Owls have very sharp beaks, which they use to rip the flesh off prey. Their incredible eyesight helps them to see prey animals in the dark.

THE SNOWY OWL

Snowy owls are beautiful birds of prey that live in cold places such as northern Canada and Alaska. They have adapted to their snowy home by becoming almost white in color. This camouflages the bird against the snow and allows it to **stalk** prey in the air almost unnoticed.

This snowy owl has excellent eyesight. It can even see white animals such as this arctic fox hiding in the snow.

Monkey Moves

Spider monkeys are the tumblers of the rain forest!
They swing between trees, eating fruits, nuts, eggs, and
spiders. Living in the treetops means they do not have
to compete with many other animals for food and space.

Swinging Along

The spider monkey has long arms with hooklike hands
and long fingers for swinging through the trees. Its
strong tail can twist and grip as tightly as its hands.
A rough patch of skin at the end of the tail helps
it to grip tightly, too. By swinging from its tail,
the monkey keeps its hands free to pick up food.

Spider monkeys rest
high up in the trees.
They also sleep in the
trees to keep safe from
any predators below.

Spider monkeys got their name because they look a little like spiders when they hang from their tails.

Future Story

FOREST IN DANGER

Spider monkeys are in danger. They need large areas of tall forests to survive. They are losing their homes to farming, and many trees are being cut down for wood. Spider monkeys are also hunted by people for food. The monkeys call noisily to each other between the trees, which makes them an easy target.

Crocodile Smile

Have you ever heard the saying "Never smile at a crocodile?" When a crocodile shows its teeth, it's not smiling back at you! It's getting ready to bite—and a crocodile's bite can be deadly.

Killer Jaws

The crocodile's mouth is adapted to grab and tear its prey. The crocodile uses its strong jaws and its 60 deadly teeth to grab prey and drag it underwater to drown it. It then spins its own body to tear off chunks of meat from its victim.

Every one of these teeth is hollow. There's a new tooth growing inside it, ready for use once the old one wears out. A crocodile may go through 3,000 teeth in its lifetime!

SUIT OF ARMOR

The crocodile has armorlike skin. It is covered in bony scales that overlap like the tiles on a roof. The scales protect the crocodile from scraping its skin on rocks or the ground. They also protect it from attacks by animals that might otherwise try to eat it.

Crocodiles can **bask** lazily on riverbanks without fear of an attack. Few animals dare to attack an animal protected by sharp teeth and a suit of armor.

Racing Cat

The cheetah is the fastest runner in the whole animal world. Its body is adapted to move very quickly over short distances. That is how it catches gazelle and other prey that other animals can't keep up with.

Built for Speed

The cheetah has a small head and narrow body. This gives it the perfect shape for speed. Its long legs and bendy backbone help it to take extra-long strides. Its legs are powered by strong muscles and its long tail helps it to balance and steer when making fast turns. The claws on its feet are hard and sharp. They grip the ground better than running shoes as the cheetah races along.

Cheetahs can run at 70 miles (100 km) per hour. That's as fast as a car on a freeway.

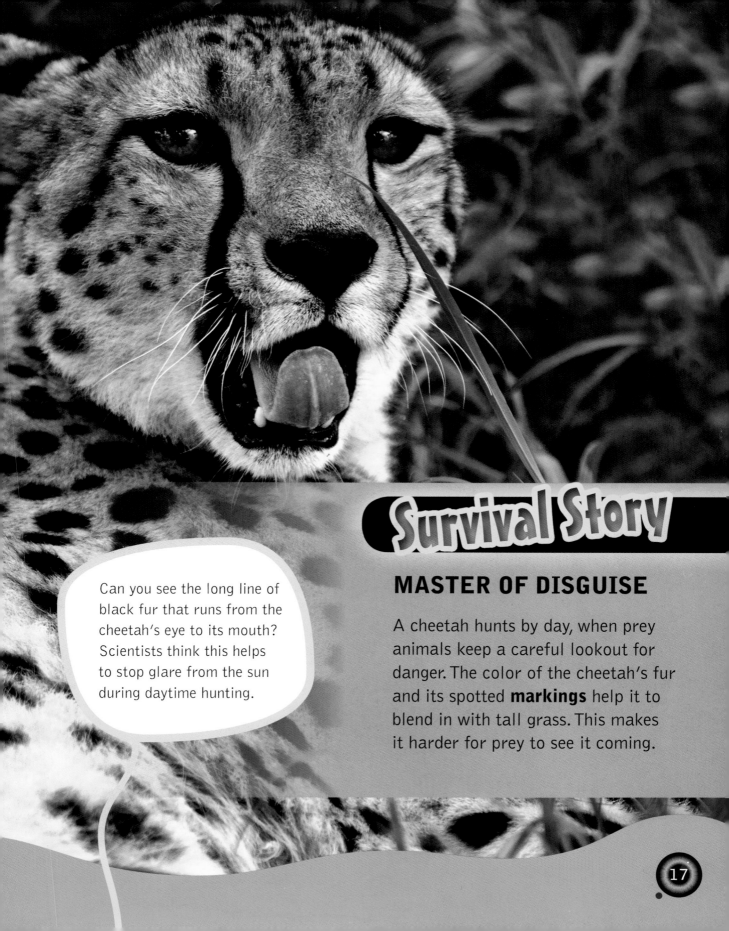

Can you see the long line of black fur that runs from the cheetah's eye to its mouth? Scientists think this helps to stop glare from the sun during daytime hunting.

Survival Story

MASTER OF DISGUISE

A cheetah hunts by day, when prey animals keep a careful lookout for danger. The color of the cheetah's fur and its spotted **markings** help it to blend in with tall grass. This makes it harder for prey to see it coming.

Chameleon Color

The chameleon can quickly change color. It can change from green to brown and back faster than you can change your shirt! It has adapted in this way to survive in its habitat.

Why Change Color?

A chameleon changes color when the light or temperature changes. It also changes color if its mood changes, such as when it is scared. Most chameleons turn green, yellow, cream, or dark brown. A chameleon's normal color is green or brown to help it to blend in with the trees it lives in. Chameleons camouflage themselves to catch their prey. They sit hidden among tree leaves and wait for prey to pass by, then shoot out their tongue to catch their meal.

A chameleon's tongue is longer than its body. It shoots out at high speed and traps insect prey on its sticky tip.

SPINNING EYEBALLS

The chameleon's eyes are amazing. Each eye can look in the opposite direction to the other eye. This lets the chameleon look at two things at the same time. If the chameleon sees a predator or prey, both eyes look in the same direction to get a clear view.

The chameleon can move its eyes to get a complete view around its whole body.

Snow Bear

The polar bear lives in the Arctic at the far north of our planet. This place is covered in ice and snow for most of the year. Incredibly, the polar bear has adapted to survive there.

Fat and Fur

The polar bear has two layers of hair. These trap warm air around its body and create a waterproof layer that stops the bear's skin from becoming wet and cold. Polar bear hair looks white but it is see-through. Sunlight passes through the hairs and is soaked up by the bear's black skin. The bear also has a 4-inch (10-cm) thick layer of **blubber** all over its body. This acts like a blanket to keep the bear warm.

The polar bear's blubber keeps it warm and helps it to float in the freezing waters of the Arctic.

MELTING ICE

The polar bear travels very long distances to find its prey, often drifting on blocks of floating ice. It dives into the water to catch seals from these icy platforms. The polar bear is in danger, though. **Global warming** is melting ice sheets and stopping polar bears from traveling in search of food.

In the future there may be fewer polar bears because the ice platforms they travel on and hunt from are melting fast.

Spider's Trap

All spiders are predators. They feed on other small animals, such as insects. Many spiders catch their prey by trapping it in their silky webs.

Spinning Silk

A spider makes webs from threads of silk. It makes silk inside its body and pushes it out from the end of its **abdomen**. When an insect lands on the web, it becomes stuck or tangled in the silk. As it struggles, the spider feels the web move and rushes out to catch its prey. Some spiders wrap prey in silk before eating it or storing it to eat later.

Spider silk is incredibly strong. It is stronger than a thread of steel of the same thickness!

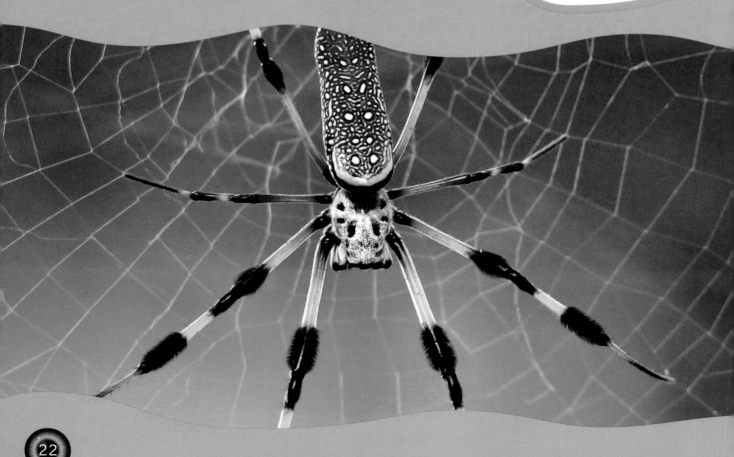

True Story

FIRING HAIR DARTS

Many animals try to eat tarantula spiders, including lizards, birds, and snakes. Some tarantulas have an adaptation to escape hungry predators. They use their legs to flick special hairs off their abdomen. These hairs stick in a predator's eyes. This gives the tarantula time to escape.

This tarantula will only attack when it feels threatened.

Snake Attack

Snakes do not have arms or legs with which to catch animals. So how do they keep prey from escaping? Some snakes **inject** their prey with a poison called **venom**.

Venom and Fangs

When a venomous snake spots an animal, it reaches forward quickly and bites with long, hollow teeth called fangs. It injects its venom through the fangs into the prey. The venom works quickly. It **paralyzes** large prey to stop it from moving, and kills smaller animals. Then the snake can swallow the prey whole, usually head first. If the prey is large, the snake can even loosen its jaw to fit it all in.

You can see the venom dripping from this snake's fangs. Snakes strike at high speed.

Pythons rest in trees by coiling their bodies around branches.

True Story

CRUSHED TO DEATH

The python does not use venom to kill prey. It grabs an animal in its teeth, coils its body around the prey, and squeezes. It squeezes so tightly that the prey animal cannot breathe. When the animal is dead, the snake loosens its jaw and swallows its prey whole.

Zebra Journey

Every year hundreds of thousands of zebras set out on an enormous journey across Africa. They **migrate** over huge distances. The zebras face dangerous predators and very deep rivers along the way. This way of traveling as a group is an adaptation that helps zebra herds to survive.

On the Move

Zebras eat grasses and drink from pools of rainwater called watering holes. During the dry season in Africa, grass plants die. Zebra herds then travel to find more food and watering holes. Crossing rivers is especially dangerous, as crocodiles lie in wait to eat the weaker animals.

Zebras often travel with wildebeest and other migrating animals so they can warn each other about predators.

Future Story

BROKEN JOURNEYS

Zebras travel up to 1,864 miles (3,000 km) on their journey. Today, many parts of Africa are broken up by villages, highways, farms, and fences. Some zebras are killed when they cross highways. Some die when their route is blocked, and they cannot get to the food or water they need in time.

Young zebras migrate with the herds. They are most at risk of death from lack of food or water.

Changing World

The world is constantly changing. People cut down trees and take over wild land for buildings, farms, and factories. Global warming is melting ice. Rivers are drying up as the land warms. How will animals cope with these changes?

Changing Quickly

Animals take thousands of years to adapt their bodies. However, some animals can adapt their behavior much more quickly in order to survive. As wild areas are lost, animals such as raccoons, foxes, and rats change their ways. Instead of living in the country, many have adapted to live in or near cities. There, they eat leftover food thrown away by people instead of wild food.

This raccoon is eating from a bird feeder. As people have taken over raccoon habitats, raccoons have adapted to live there too. They even eat from garbage cans.

True Story

BAMBOO EATER

The giant panda is adapted to eat only bamboo. Its head is huge to hold the powerful jaw muscles it needs to chew this tough plant. However, because it eats only one type of food, the panda is in danger. Bamboo forests have been cut down and highways and villages now block many panda paths to other forests.

Although giant pandas are **endangered** animals, the Chinese government is creating panda **reserves** where they can live safely.

Glossary

abdomen: the part of the body that contains the stomach and gut

adaptation: the slow process of change that helps animals and plants to survive in their environments

bask: to lie in the sun to soak up its warmth

blubber: a thick layer of fat beneath an animal's skin. Blubber helps an animal to keep warm

camouflage: body patterns or colors that help animals blend in with their surroundings

compete: to try to be the best, or to try to beat another

endangered: in danger of dying out

global warming: a rise in Earth's temperature

habitat: the place in which an animal lives

inflate: to fill with air

inject: to make a hole in the surface of an animal's skin and to then push a liquid into its body

markings: the patterns on an animal's body

mate: one of two animals that come together to produce babies

migrate: when an animal travels from place to place in order to find food or to have babies

paralyze: to stop something moving

predator: animal that hunts and eats other animals

prey: an animal that is eaten by other animals

reserve: place in which animals can live safely

stalk: to hide from an animal while hunting it

venom: poisonous liquid that some animals use to kill other animals

For More Information

Books

Parker, Steve. *Extreme Animals.* Hauppauge, NY: Barron's Educational Series, 2009.

Slade, Suzanne.*What Do You Know about Animal Adaptations?* New York, NY: PowerKids Press, 2008.

Townsend, John. *Amazing Animal Survivors.* Chicago, IL: Raintree, 2013.

Websites

Visit this website to play a matching game about animal adaptations.
www.ecokids.ca/pub/eco_info/topics/climate/adaptations/index.cfm

Find out more about all sorts of animal and plant adaptations.
www.bbc.co.uk/nature/adaptations

Pick an animal from the list on the right to find out all about it and how it is adapted to its habitat.
animals.nationalgeographic.com/animals

Index